What's what?
Birds

Written by Ruth Thomson
Illustrated by Maurice Pledger

Contents

Watts Books

London · New York · Sydney

What's a bird?

There are thousands of sorts of birds of all shapes, sizes and colours. They have these things in common.

All birds are covered with feathers.

All birds have two wings, but they can't all fly.

All birds have a tail. It is used for steering in flight.

All birds have a hard beak.

All birds have two legs and feet with toes.

All female birds lay eggs.

nest

2

sparrowhawk

Birds fly by flapping
their wings up and down.

Birds' bones are hollow
and full of air.
This makes them
light enough to fly.

wagtail

sparrow

3

Who's who?

You can often recognise a bird by its shape. Can you match these shapes with the birds on the opposite page?

mallard

wren

grey
heron

puffin

Canada
goose

swallow

Adélie
penguin

kingfisher

buzzard

little
owl

hawfinch

Beaks

Birds have hard beaks instead of teeth. A bird's beak suits the food it eats.

curlew

Seed eaters have short, tough beaks.

Wading birds have long beaks for grabbing worms and other animals out of the mud.

Insect eaters have thin, pointed beaks.

Birds of prey have strong, hooked beaks for tearing meat.

swallow

eagle

6

hummingbird

Nectar eaters have very long, thin beaks to reach inside flowers.

blackbird

Some birds have tweezer beaks. They are pointed for picking up seeds and long enough to grasp worms.

Ducks have flattened beaks for filtering food from water.

shoveler

what's what?

What do these birds eat?

kestrel

godwit

sparrow

nightjar

Open the flap to find out.

Feathers

Feathers keep birds warm
and dry. They help them to fly.

Fluffy down feathers
lie next to a bird's skin.
They trap air which
keeps the bird warm.

*body
feather*

down feather

Body feathers overlap smoothly
on top of the down feathers. They are oily
and waterproof. They keep the bird dry.

wing feather

Wing feathers are long, stiff and strong.
They are very light. Each one is shaped
slightly differently to help the bird to fly.

8

Birds comb their feathers
with their beaks to get rid
of dust and insects.
This is called
preening.

Worn out feathers fall out
from time to time.
New ones grow in their place.
This is called moulting.

What's what?

Whose feathers are these:

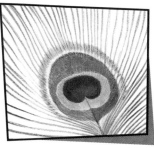

a pheasant's or a peacock's?

a pigeon's or a parrot's?

a swan's or a guinea fowl's?

a flamingo's or a blackbird's?

Open the flap to find out.

Wings

A bird's wings are rounded on top and nearly flat underneath. Their shape helps to lift the bird into the air when it flaps its wings.

Fast flying birds have pointed wings that curve backwards.

swift

Seabirds have long, narrow wings for gliding miles and miles.

fulmar

10

Birds of prey have long, wide wings for soaring high in the sky.

golden eagle

Woodland birds have short, wide wings for twisting and dodging between trees.

pheasant

What's what?

Which wing is good for:
- flying fast ?
- gliding long distances?
- soaring high in the sky?
- dodging between trees?

Feet

Birds have feet that suit the place where they live and feed.

swan

swan's foot

Swimming birds have webbed feet. They push against the water like a paddle.

Garden birds have four toes, three in front and one behind, so they can grasp branches.

greenfinch's foot

greenfinch

12

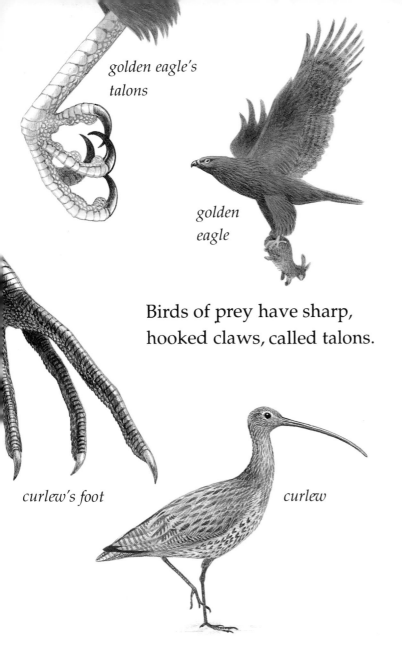

golden eagle's talons

golden eagle

Birds of prey have sharp, hooked claws, called talons.

curlew's foot

curlew

Birds in muddy places have long toes for walking. These spread out wide so the bird doesn't sink.

what's what?

Which foot is used for:

- swimming?
- perching?
- catching prey?
- walking?

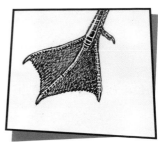

Open the flap to find out.

Nests

All birds lay eggs from which their young hatch. Most birds build nests to protect them. They make nests of all sorts of things.

The house martin builds a nest of mud.

The crow makes a nest of twigs.

The lark weaves a nest of grass.

The dabchick builds a nest of rotting reeds.

The chaffinch makes
a nest of moss and lichen
and lines it with feathers
and hair.

The green woodpecker
nests in tree holes.

The razorbill
lays its eggs on
the rocky ledge
of a steep cliff.

The little tern makes a hollow
for its eggs on a sandy beach.

Eggs

Birds' eggs are all different colours and sizes. Some are almost round, others have a pointed end.

tawny owl

cormorant

emu

kiwi

Eggs laid in holes are usually white.

sand martin

nightingale

chickadee

ringed plover

wood warbler

pelican

guillemot

jackdaw

song thrush

Eggs laid in nests in the open are speckled. They are hard to see.

The mother bird
sits on the eggs
to keep them warm
until the chicks hatch.

common tern

The chick in this egg
is ready to hatch.
It has chipped a hole
in the eggshell.

The chick pushes its way out.
Hatching is hard work.
It takes hours or even days.

common tern chick

Chicks

Chicks that hatch in nests
in trees are naked, blind
and helpless. Chicks that
hatch in nests on the ground
are covered with down.

The chicks are always hungry.
Their parents feed them all the time.
The young birds grow very fast.
When their feathers have grown,
they learn to fly.

song thrush

Chicks that hatch
on the ground
can usually soon walk
and busily find food
for themselves.

*mother hen
and chicks*

At night, they keep warm
under their mother's wings.

Whose chicks are these?

Emperor penguin   mute swan

snowy owl   partridge

Open the flap to find out.

Record holders

The largest bird

An ostrich may be over 2.5m tall and weigh over 150kg. It cannot fly.

ostrich

The smallest bird

 bee hummingbird

The bee hummingbird is about the size of a grown-up's thumb. It weighs less than a large moth.

The most common wild bird

red-billed quelea

**The bird that flies
the furthest**

The Arctic tern goes from
the Arctic to the tip of South Africa.

Arctic tern

**The bird with
the widest wingspan**

The wandering albatross
has wings which spread
over 3.5m wide.

wandering albatross

**The bird with the
biggest beak**

Toco toucan

Bird quiz

What can you remember?
Look back through the book
to help you find the answers.

1. Do birds have teeth?

a   b c

2. Whose foot is this?

3. Can you name these three feathers?

4. How do birds fly?

5. Whose nest is this?

6. Whose egg is this?

7. Which three birds make up this strange looking bird?

8. Which bird is the odd one out?

buzzard

owl

pigeon

eagle

Bird Words

Created by
Thumbprint Books,
77 Barnsbury St,
London N1 1EJ

© 1994 Thumbprint Books

First published in 1994 by
Watts Books
96 Leonard Street
London EC2A 4RH

Franklin Watts Australia
14 Mars Road
Lane Cove NSW 2066

Designer: Roger Hands
Consultant: Michael Chinery

A CIP catalogue record for this
book is available from
the British Library.
Dewey Decimal Classification: 598

ISBN 0 7496 1646 6 (hardback)
ISBN 0 7496 1856 6 (paperback)

10 9 8 7 6 5 4 3 2 1

Printed in Hong Kong